161 IMAGES

Front: Jonny and Jaimie, *Mayerling*
Inside front: Tamara, *Carmen*
Inside back: Jaimie and Yohei, *The Nutcracker*
Back flap: Johan, backstage at the Bolshoi
Back: Johanna Adams, *Swan Lake*

THE ROYAL BALLET

161 IMAGES

BY JOHAN PERSSON

OBERON BOOKS

LONDON

Published in 2003 by the Royal Opera House
in association with Oberon Books Ltd

Oberon Books (incorporating Absolute Classics)
521 Caledonian Road, London N7 9RH
Tel: 020 7607 Fax: 020 7607 3629
oberon.books@btinternet.com
www.oberonbooks.com

ISBN: 1 84002 374 0

Cover and book design: Jeff Willis
and Andrzej Klimowski

Printed in Great Britain by G&B Printers, Hanworth,
Middlesex

Johan Persson would like to acknowledge: Tony Hall,
Monica Mason and especially the staff and dancers of
The Royal Ballet. With much love and respect, Johan.
johanpersson@apik.net

TO MY FRIENDS AND COLLEAGUES
AT THE ROYAL BALLET

Monica Mason and Roberto

Manon

I am delighted to have the opportunity to introduce this first book of photographs by Johan Persson. Johan, who until last year was a Principal dancer with the Company, has long combined a successful career as a performer with his other great interest – photography. His photographs of The Royal Ballet show a unique and personal perspective of the Company at work and the talent and skills that he possessed as a dancer are equally apparent in his photographs. His eye and sense of timing create arresting and beautiful images and he has been able to photograph the dancers in a way that demonstrates the closeness and familiarity he still enjoys with his former colleagues.

This book marks the start of a new career for Johan which shows every sign of being as accomplished as his first. I wish him every possible success.

MONICA MASON

Darcey

Romeo and Juliet

Dance and photography have been my two great passions since childhood, so when a knee injury put an early end to my career as a dancer I turned naturally to my camera. Having photographed dance for many years, I was given the opportunity to record moments from the working lives of dancers from The Royal Ballet during the 2002/3 Season.

The private, behind-the-scenes world of an internationally renowned Company such as The Royal Ballet is fascinating territory for a photographer and I wanted to capture that world as I know it. *161 Images* is the result. It is an intimate portrait, recording moments of exhilaration, exhaustion, intense pressure and relaxation, illustrating the talent and total commitment of the artists who make this unique Company what it is.

JOHAN PERSSON

Alina

Mayerling

Johan and Alina   *Mayerling*

Johan and Monica Parker

Mayerling

Alina, Johan and Lynn Seymour   *Mayerling*

Elizabeth

Mayerling

Johan and Bethany   *Mayerling*

Genesia and Robert   *Mayerling*

Monica, Robert and Laura

Mayerling

Zen and Jonny

Mayerling

Johan   *Mayerling*

Alina   *Mayerling*

Jonny

Mayerling

Mara and Robert

Mayerling

Mara and Robert

Mayerling

Robert   *Mayerling*

Mark Morris   *Gong*

Ricardo   *Gong*

Bella   *Gong*

Christopher Wheeldon

Tryst

Dancers

Tryst

Mats Ek

Carmen

Jaimie and Mats Ek   *Carmen*

Mats Ek and Edward   *Carmen*

Tom and Tamara   *Carmen*

Zen and Tom

Carmen

Bennet

Carmen

Massimo

Carmen

Jonny   *Carmen*

Tamara

Carmen

Tamara

Carmen

Jaimie   *Carmen*

Tom   *Carmen*

Will

The Wind in the Willows

Iohna

The Wind in the Willows

Gail

Swan Lake

Iohna

Swan Lake

The Company

Swan Lake

Zen

Swan Lake

Zen

Swan Lake

Jaimie

Swan Lake

Will

Swan Lake

Isabel

Swan Lake

Edward

The Nutcracker

Helen

Sian

The Nutcracker

Ryoichi

The Nutcracker

Johannes

The Nutcracker

Briony and Kristen

The Nutcracker

Johan and Alexander Agadzhanov

The Nutcracker

Ernst

The Nutcracker

Darcey and Ryoichi

The Nutcracker

Yohei, Lesley Collier and Jaimie

The Nutcracker

Jaimie

The Nutcracker

John

The Nutcracker

Maurice

The Nutcracker

Samantha

The Nutcracker

SINFONIETTA, choreography Jiří Kylián

Laura

Sinfonietta

Martin   *Sinfonietta*

Jiří Kylián

Sinfonietta

Emma

Sinfonietta

Samantha

Scènes de ballet

Kenta and Deirdre

Scènes de ballet

Alastair and Jane

Winter Dreams

Sir Anthony

Winter Dreams

Sir Anthony   *Winter Dreams*

Nicolas

Winter Dreams

Nicolas   *Winter Dreams*

Sir Anthony and the Company

Winter Dreams

Brian   *Manon*

Brian   *Manon*

David and Martin   *Manon*

Philip

Manon

Darcey

Manon

Alastair   *Manon*

David and Jaimie   *Manon*

Jaimie and David   *Manon*

David and Monica

Manon

Helen

Manon

Fran and Tomoko   *Manon*

Martin

Manon

Elizabeth

Manon

Vanessa   *Manon*

Natalia Makarova

The Sleeping Beauty

Miyako

The Sleeping Beauty

Johan and Miyako   *The Sleeping Beauty*

Tom

The Sleeping Beauty

Edward and Jochen Pahs

The Sleeping Beauty

Marianela

The Sleeping Beauty

Yohei

The Sleeping Beauty

Isabel

The Sleeping Beauty

Christina

The Sleeping Beauty

Jane   *The Sleeping Beauty*

Gemma

The Sleeping Beauty

Ryoichi

The Sleeping Beauty

José

The Sleeping Beauty

Vicky

The Sleeping Beauty

Natasha

The Sleeping Beauty

Emma and the Wolf

The Sleeping Beauty

Edward

The Sleeping Beauty

The Hunt scene

The Sleeping Beauty

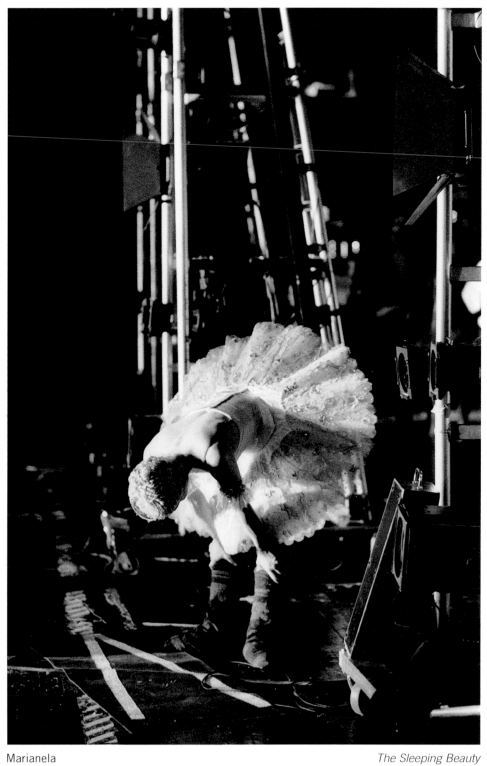

Marianela

The Sleeping Beauty

Yohei   *The Sleeping Beauty*

Monica and Isabel

The Sleeping Beauty

APOLLO, choreography George Balanchine

Roberto

Apollo

Deirdre and Patricia Neary   *Apollo*

Carlos   *Apollo*

Roberto   *Apollo*

Roberto and Patricia Neary *Apollo*

Carlos

Apollo

Tetsuya

Le Corsaire

Tamara and Edward   *Images of Love*

Edward   *Images of Love*

Carlos

Gloria

Carlos   *Gloria*

Valeri   *Gloria*

The Company

Monica

Gloria

Irek   *The Judas Tree*

Mara   *The Judas Tree*

Jonny

The Judas Tree

David Bintley   *Les Saisons*

Emma   *Les Saisons*

William and Ricardo

Romeo and Juliet

Michael

Romeo and Juliet

Ricardo

Romeo and Juliet

Chris

Romeo and Juliet

Ivan

A Month in the Country

Yu Hui

Body conditioning

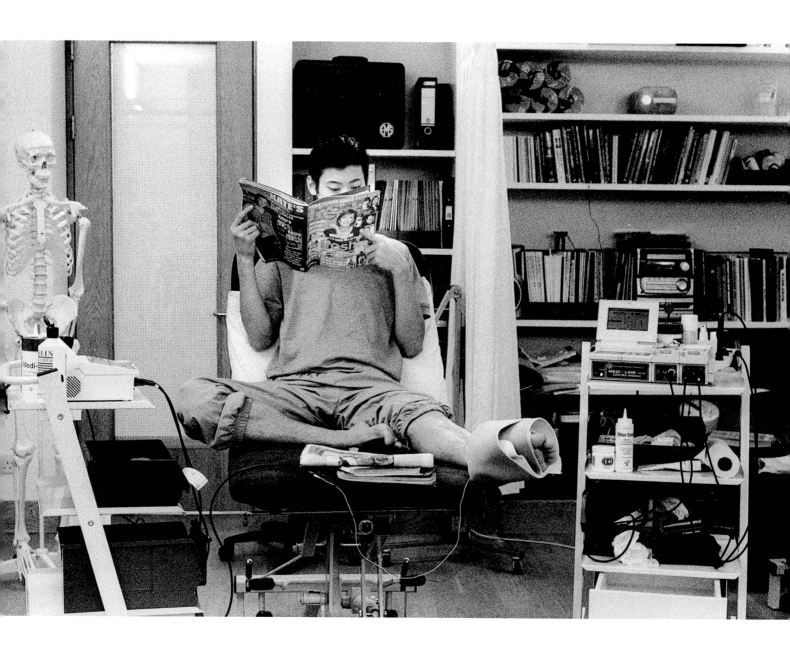

Ryoichi

Physiotherapy

Jane

Gillie

Nathan

Physiotherapy

Darcey

Dancers' lounge

Johan

Moscow Airport

Ivan

Bus

Isabel, Laura, Christina and Josh   *Outside the theatre*

Swans

Alexander Agadzhanov and Tamara

On stage

Marianela

Tamara and Carlos

Jaimie

On stage

Oliver and Iñaki

Dressing room

Zen

Dressing room

Iohna

On stage

Irek and Tamara

Winter Dreams

Miyako

La Fille mal gardée

Carlos

Le Corsaire

Carlos

Stage door

Laura and Ricardo

The Kremlin

PHOTOGRAPH INDEX

Front   Jonathan Cope and Jaimie Tapper rehearsing for the roles of Crown Prince Rudolf and Countess Marie Larisch in *Mayerling* in the Ashton Studio.

Inside   Tamara Rojo rehearsing Carmen in the Ashton Studio.

6   Monica Mason coaching Roberto Bolle for the role of Des Grieux in *Manon* in the De Valois Studio.

8   Darcey Bussell rehearsing Juliet on stage.

MAYERLING, choreography Sir Kenneth MacMillan

10   Alina Cojocaru rehearsing Mary Vetsera in the Clore Studio Upstairs.

11   Johan Kobborg and Alina Cojocaru rehearsing Crown Prince Rudolf and Mary Vetsera in the Clore Studio Upstairs.

12   Johan Kobborg with ballet notator Monica Parker rehearsing *Mayerling* in the De Valois Studio.

13   Lynn Seymour coaching Johan Kobborg and Alina Cojocaru for Crown Prince Rudolf and Mary Vetsera in the Clore Studio Upstairs.

14   Elizabeth McGorian rehearsing Empress Elisabeth in the De Valois Studio.

15   Johan Kobborg and Bethany Keating rehearsing Crown Prince Rudolf and Princess Stephanie in the De Valois Studio.

16   Genesia Rosato and Robert Tewsley rehearsing Countess Marie Larisch and Crown Prince Rudolf in the De Valois Studio.

17   Monica Mason giving notes to Robert Tewsley and Laura Morera in the De Valois Studio.

18   Zenaida Yanowsky and Jonathan Cope rehearsing Empress Elisabeth and Crown Prince Rudolf in the Fonteyn Studio.

19   Johan Kobborg rehearsing Crown Prince Rudolf on stage.

20   Alina Cojocaru in the MacMillan Studio before going on stage to dance Mary Vetsera.

21   Jonathan Cope performing Crown Prince Rudolf.

22   Mara Galeazzi and Robert Tewsley rehearsing Mary Vetsera and Crown Prince Rudolf on stage.

23   Mara Galeazzi and Robert Tewsley rehearsing Mary Vetsera and Crown Prince Rudolf on stage.

24   Robert Tewsley as Crown Prince Rudolf on stage.

GONG, choreography Mark Morris

25   Mark Morris rehearsing his ballet on stage.

26   Ricardo Cervera rehearsing on stage.

27   Belinda Hatley in her dressing room.

TRYST, choreography Christopher Wheeldon

28   Christopher Wheeldon choreographing in the Fonteyn Studio.

29   Dancers in rehearsal on stage.

CARMEN, choreography Mats Ek

30   Mats Ek demonstrating in the Ashton Studio.

31   Mats Ek rehearsing Jaimie Tapper in the Ashton Studio.

32   Mats Ek and Edward Watson rehearsing in the Ashton Studio.

33   Thomas Whitehead and Tamara Rojo rehearsing in the Ashton Studio.

34   Zenaida Yanowsky and Thomas Whitehead rehearsing in the Ashton Studio.

35   Bennet Gartside resting in the Ashton Studio.

36   Massimo Murru in performance.

37   Jonathan Cope in performance.

38   Tamara Rojo in performance.

39   Tamara Rojo in performance.

40   Jaimie Tapper in performance.

41   Thomas Whitehead in performance.

THE WIND IN THE WILLOWS, choreography William Tuckett

42   William Tuckett choreographing in the Fonteyn Studio.

43   Iohna Loots as Rabbit in the Linbury Studio Theatre.

SWAN LAKE, choreography Marius Petipa and Lev Ivanov

44   Ballet Mistress Gail Taphouse taking a rehearsal in the De Valois Studio.

45   Iohna Loots rehearsing in the De Valois Studio.

46   Members of The Royal Ballet preparing for rehearsal on stage.

47   Zenaida Yanowsky in her dressing room.

48   Zenaida Yanowsky as Odette in performance.

49   Jaimie Tapper between Act I and Act II.

50   William Tuckett in performance as Von Rothbart.

51   Isabel McMeekan in performance.

THE NUTCRACKER, choreography Sir Peter Wright after Lev Ivanov

52   Edward Watson in the De Valois Studio during rehearsal.

53   Helen Crawford in the De Valois Studio.

54   Sian Murphy resting in the De Valois Studio.

55   Ryoichi Hirano on the balcony between acts.

56   Johannes Stepanek waiting backstage between acts.

57   Briony Viele and Kristen McGarrity, two students from the Royal Ballet School, before Act II.

58   Johan Kobborg with Principal Répétiteur Alexander Agadzhanov before the curtain goes up on Act II.

59   Ernst Meisner in the wings.

60   Darcey Bussell and Ryoichi Hirano backstage before Act II.

61   Lesley Collier giving corrections to Jaimie Tapper and Yohei Sasaki after a rehearsal on stage.

62   Jaimie Tapper in the wings.

63   Jonathan Howells as the Prince.

64   Maurice Vodegel-Matzen in the Arabian dance.

65   Samantha Raine in the wings.

SINFONIETTA, choreography Jiří Kylián

66   Laura Morera rehearsing in the Fonteyn Studio.

67   Martin Harvey rehearsing in the Fonteyn Studio.

68   Jiří Kylián rehearsing his ballet in the Fonteyn Studio.

69   Emma Maguire rehearsing in the Fonteyn Studio.

SCÈNES DE BALLET, choreography Sir Frederick Ashton

70   Samantha Raine rehearsing in the De Valois studio.

71   Kenta Kura and Deirdre Chapman before rehearsal in the De Valois Studio.

WINTER DREAMS, choreography Sir Kenneth MacMillan

72   Alastair Marriott and Jane Burn rehearsing in the Fonteyn Studio.

73   Sir Anthony Dowell rehearsing in the Fonteyn Studio.

74   Sir Anthony Dowell rehearsing in the Fonteyn Studio.

75   Nicolas Le Riche rehearsing in the Fonteyn Studio.

76   Nicolas Le Riche rehearsing in the Fonteyn Studio.

77   Sir Anthony Dowell and the Company after a rehearsal on stage.

MANON, choreography Sir Kenneth MacMillan

78   Brian Maloney rehearsing Lescaut in the De Valois Studio.

79   Brian Maloney rehearsing Lescaut in the De Valois Studio.

80   David Drew and Martin Harvey rehearsing Monsieur G M and Lescaut in the De Valois Studio.

81   Philip Mosley rehearsing the Old Man in the De Valois Studio.

82   Darcey Bussell rehearsing Manon in the De Valois Studio.

83   Alastair Marriott rehearsing the Old Man in the De Valois Studio.

84   David Makhateli and Jaimie Tapper rehearsing Des Grieux and Manon in the De Valois Studio.

85   Jaimie Tapper and David Makhateli rehearsing Manon and Des Grieux in the De Valois Studio.

86   Monica Mason giving David Makhateli a correction for the role of Des Grieux in the De Valois Studio.

87   Helen Crawford in the dressing room before Act II.

88   Francesca Filpi and Tomoko Furuya in their dressing rooms before Act II.

89   Martin Harvey as Lescaut in Act I.

90   Elizabeth McGorian as Madame in Act II.

91   Vanessa Palmer as Lescaut's Mistress in Act II.

THE SLEEPING BEAUTY, choreography Marius Petipa

92   Natalia Makarova setting *The Sleeping Beauty* in the De Valois Studio.

93   Miyako Yoshida rehearsing Aurora in the De Valois Studio.

94   Johan Kobborg and Miyako Yoshida rehearsing in the De Valois Studio.

95   Thomas Whitehead watching a rehearsal in the De Valois Studio.

96   Jochen Pahs applying Carabosse make-up to Edward Watson.

97   Marianela Nuñez in her dressing room before a performance.

98   Yohei Sasaki warming up in the MacMillan Studio.

99   Isabel McMeekan on the balcony before a performance.

100   Christina Elida Salerno warming up in the MacMillan Studio before a performance.

101   Jane Burn warming up on stage before a performance.

102   Gemma Bond as Cinderella in the wings.

103   Ryoichi Hirano backstage.

104   José Martín as Bluebird in the wings.

105   Victoria Hewitt backstage.

106   Natasha Oughtred as the White Cat backstage.

107   Emma Maguire backstage with the Wolf (David Pickering).

108   Edward Watson as Carabosse backstage.

109   Before the curtain goes up on the Hunt scene in Act II.

110   Marianela Nuñez as Princess Aurora before going on stage.

111   Yohei Sasaki backstage after finishing the Bluebird solo.

112   Monica Mason speaking with Isabel McMeekan after the final *Sleeping Beauty* performance of the season.

APOLLO, choreography George Balanchine

113   Roberto Bolle rehearsing Apollo in the MacMillan Studio.

114   Deirdre Chapman rehearsing Polyhymnia with Balanchine répétiteur Patricia Neary in the MacMillan Studio.

115   Carlos Acosta rehearsing Apollo in the Fonteyn Studio.

116   Roberto Bolle rehearsing Apollo in the MacMillan Studio.

117   Patricia Neary demonstrating a step from Apollo for Roberto Bolle in the MacMillan Studio.

118   Carlos Acosta rehearsing on stage for Apollo.

LE CORSAIRE, choreography after Marius Petipa

119   Tetsuya Kumakawa resting in the Fonteyn Studio after finishing his variation.

IMAGES OF LOVE, choreography Sir Kenneth MacMillan

120   Tamara Rojo and Edward Watson rehearsing in the De Valois Studio.

121   Edward Watson rehearsing in the De Valois Studio.

GLORIA, choreography Sir Kenneth MacMillan

122   Carlos Acosta rehearsing on stage.

124   Carlos Acosta rehearsing backstage.

125   Valeri Hristov waiting backstage before a performance.

126   Members of the Company in rehearsal for *Gloria* on stage.

127   Monica Mason on stage following a rehearsal.

THE JUDAS TREE, choreography Sir Kenneth MacMillan

128   Irek Mukhamedov rehearsing in the De Valois Studio.

129   Mara Galeazzi on stage.

130   Jonathan Cope on stage in a final rehearsal.

LES SAISONS, choreography David Bintley

131   David Bintley in the Fonteyn Studio creating his ballet.

132   Emma Maguire outside the Fonteyn Studio during a break from rehearsal.

ROMEO AND JULIET, choreography Sir Kenneth MacMillan

133   William Tuckett and Ricardo Cervera as Tybalt and Mercutio in the Fonteyn Studio.

134   Michael Stojko rehearsing the sword fights in the Fonteyn Studio.

135   Ricardo Cervera rehearsing Mercutio in the Fonteyn Studio.

136   Christopher Saunders in performance as Tybalt.

A MONTH IN THE COUNTRY, choreography Sir Frederick Ashton

137   Ivan Putrov in rehearsal in the Ashton studio. The ballet was performed on the Russian tour, 2003.

IN PREPARATION

138   Yu Hui Choe, stretching in the body-conditioning room.

139   Ryoichi Hirano receiving treatment in the physiotherapy room.

140   Jane Paris, Body Control Instructor, in the body-conditioning room.

141   Mother-to-be Gillian Revie taking class in the De Valois Studio.

142   Nathan Coppen in the physiotherapy room.

143   Darcey Bussell preparing her shoes in the dancers' lounge.

MOSCOW

144   Johan Kobborg waiting for the bus at Moscow Airport.

145   Ivan Putrov on the bus to the hotel after arriving at the airport.

THE BOLSHOI THEATRE

146   Laura Morera, Christina Elida Salerno, Isabel McMeekan and Joshua Tuifua waiting for the bus outside the theatre.

147   Swans making their crossover backstage.

148   Alexander Agadzhanov rehearsing Tamara Rojo for *Swan Lake* on stage.

150   Marianela Nuñez rehearsing Kitri from *Don Quixote* in Studio 1.

151   Tamara Rojo and Carlos Acosta rehearsing a *pas de deux* from *Manon* in Studio 2.

152   Jaimie Tapper on stage.

153   Oliver Greatrex and Iñaki Urlezaga before a performance of *Gloria*.

154   Zenaida Yanowsky having her hat pinned in before *Mayerling*.

155   Iohna Loots before Act II of *Mayerling*.

156   Irek Mukhamedov and Tamara Rojo performing a *pas de deux* from *Winter Dreams*.

157   Miyako Yoshida performing an excerpt from *La Fille mal gardée*, choreography Sir Frederick Ashton.

158   Carlos Acosta performing *Le Corsaire*.

159   Carlos Acosta signing programmes by the stage door.

160   Ricardo Cervera and Laura Morera at the Kremlin on their day off.

Flap   Johan Persson backstage at the Bolshoi Theatre.

Inside   Jaimie Tapper and Yohei Sasaki on stage after a rehearsal of *The Nutcracker*.

Back   Stage Manager Johanna Adams checking the lights before Act II of *Swan Lake*.